TABLE OF CONTENTS

Introduction

On 1 October, 2009, the People's Republic of China (PRC) celebrated the 60th year of its independence with a parade of modern military equipment that included the full panoply of mechanized armored vehicles, fighter jets, and missile forces. The People's Liberation Army (PLA)[1] that was once a peasant-based, poorly equipped revolutionary force was now a modernized military force with joint capabilities. Also, earlier that year on 23 April, the PLA Navy conducted a naval parade off the waters of Qindao in celebration of the Navy's 60th anniversary. However, the PRC's military achievements are small compared to tremendous growth of its economy since the late 1970s when Deng Xiaoping, Chairman of the Chinese Communist Party (CCP), made economic modernization a priority with his policy of the "Four Modernizations."[2]

China's rise was not a secret to anyone. Academics and analysts tracked the military and economic growth of the "Middle Kingdom" with great interest for at least the last thirty years. In the late 1990s, many academic and military analysts speculated on China's ambitions and efforts to modernize its military capabilities. In 1997, reporter Bill Gertz captured the sentiment of many when he penned his book *The China Threat: How the People's Republic Targets America*. More recently, the U.S. Department of Defense, in its annual report to Congress on the PRC's military power, expressed concern over the "uncertainty" of China's course "particularly regarding how

---

[1] The term People's Liberation Army often includes all the military branches of service to include the ground force, air force, and navy. When referring to individual services the following terms and their acronyms are typically used: PLA Ground Forces (PLAGF), PLA Air Force (PLAAF), and PLA Navy (PLAN).

[2] The policy of "Four Modernizations" called for modernization in agriculture, industry, science and technology, and national defense. It is important to note that national defense is fourth on the list of modernizations. During the 1980s and 1990s, the armed forces of the PLA had to rely on their own efforts to generate revenue for equipment development and modernization.

its expanding military power might be used."[3] Additionally, the Joint Forces Command's *Joint Operating Environment (JOE) 2010* describes the PRC as both a potential partner and a potential threat—not just to the US, but to global peace and stability. The document states that China's strategic choices will determine "whether it will be 'another bloody century,' or one of peaceful cooperation."[4] Much of this uncertainty is due to the either intentional or unintentional strategic ambiguity of the PRC. On the one hand, the PRC is extremely secretive and many official internal documents are unavailable to other nations. On the other hand, the *JOE 2010* notes that the "Chinese themselves are uncertain as to where their strategic path to the future will lead."[5] However, there is a third component that contributes to the strategic ambiguity: the comparatively weak US understanding of Chinese strategy and military thinking. When compared to aggressive Chinese attempts to understand Western strategic thinking, this gap in understanding becomes a significant concern for US strategists. The *JOE 2010* states that in 2000, the PLA had more senior officers in US graduate degree programs than the US military, and adds that the Chinese "could understand America and its strengths and weaknesses far better than Americans understand the Chinese."[6]

China is sensitive to Western and Asian perception of its military and economic growth and has gone to great lengths to not be seen as a rising power. Since the 1990s, Chinese leaders and strategists have used the word "development" as a euphemism to describe their growth. This

---

[3] United States Department of Defense, *Annual Report to Congress: Military Power of the People's Republic of China 2008*, (Washington, D.C.: Office of the Secretary of Defense, 2008), I.

[4] United States Joint Forces Command (JFCOM), *The Joint Operating Environment 2010: Challenges and Implications for the Future Joint Force*, (Suffolk, VA: JFCOM, Center for Joint Futures, 2010), 40.

[5] Ibid.

[6] Ibid.

was in the spirit of Deng's pronouncement to "hide brightness and nourish obscurity," which is more commonly known as "bide our time and build our capabilities." However, in using euphemisms and careful wording, China may have created the conditions for increased miscalculation and misunderstanding. It is no wonder that reporters like Gertz saw China's veiled approach as an indication of hostile intent toward the US and its allies. It is very difficult to gain the trust of other nations and their leaders when your classical texts on military strategy emphasize the role of deception in war and politics.

This monograph will examine the ambiguities of Chinese strategic and military thought by introducing a new concept of *Chinese Strategic Art* to help analysts understand how the PRC thinks about and applies strategy and military capabilities. The level of analysis will be constrained to strategic level leadership of the CCP and the PLA. Unlike in the US military, where there is a tendency to separate the military from the politics, in China the PLA is the CCP's military apparatus. This study focuses on the strategic level of warfare and will not delve deeply into specific battles for the case studies. The reason for this strategic focus is to understand the conditions that influence Chinese leaders' decisions to use armed force to resolve a conflict and the level of risk that it is willing to accept. A Chinese proverb states "stones of other hills may serve to polish the jade of this one."[7] The author hopes that through this study of the Chinese strategic approach, American strategists may polish not only their understanding of Chinese strategy but their own understanding of and approach to U.S. strategy.

---

[7] Lai, David, "Learning from the Stones: A Go Approach to Mastering China's Strategic Concept, Shi," (Carlisle, PA: Strategic Studies Institute, 2004), 27.

One of the goals of this monograph is to spur discourse over the nature of strategy with "Chinese characteristics."[8] This study acknowledges that the PRC and the PLA are not monolithic, homogeneous entities, and that one must be cautious of the dangers of over generalization. However, there are certain values and attitudes within the Chinese culture that persisted over time from the dynastic periods to the modern republic. These Chinese cultural norms influenced and informed the evolution of a distinct Chinese strategic culture. The *JOE 2010* document acknowledges the influence of classical Chinese thought on recent developments in the PLA's capabilities, stating, "If one examines their emerging military capabilities in intelligence, submarines, cyber and space, one sees an asymmetrical operational approach that is different from Western approaches, one consistent with the classical Chinese strategic thinkers."[9] What, then, are the characteristics of this distinct Chinese approach?

This study reviews a multi-disciplinary selection of military, philosophical, and psychological literature to define and understand Chinese traditional and strategic culture, and the PLA's strategic theory in order to lay the foundation for developing the concept of Chinese Strategic Art. This monograph argues that there is a distinct Chinese strategic culture which combines with the principles of the strategic theory to create a unique Chinese Strategic Art. Within the Chinese Strategic Art framework are culturally distinct elements which influence the manifestation of Chinese strategy and stratagem. The Chinese Strategic Art approach is the creation and application of a strategy or stratagem that allows an inferior force to defeat a

---

[8] The term "Chinese characteristics" appears frequently in official PLA and PRC publications. The Chinese often use the term to refer to the particular social, economic, political, and cultural conditions and considerations that are unique to China. The concept harkens back to Mao Zedong's writings on strategy when he advised that Chinese Communists should study the laws and principles of revolutionary war and then modify and apply them to meet China's specific conditions.

[9] *Joint Operating Environment, 2010*, 40.

superior force. When and if the PRC does resort to armed force to solve a conflict, it is likely to do so on its own terms and in a manner that gives it an asymmetric advantage over its adversary. US strategists must bear in mind that the characteristics of the Chinese strategic approach will most likely bear little resemblance to anything to which they are accustomed. A quote attributed to the PRC's first Chairman, Mao Zedong, captures the essence of this distinct approach, "You fight in your way and we shall fight in ours."[10]

This monograph has three major sections. The first section focuses on the cultural influences on Chinese thought and Chinese strategic culture. This section provides a broad review of the differences between Western and Chinese thought and develops the argument for understanding the distinct Chinese approach to strategy. The second section develops the concept of Chinese Strategic Art, mentioned above, and describes its elements. The third section applies the Chinese Strategic Art concept to the following three case studies: the Korean War, the Sino-Vietnamese War, and the conflict with Taiwan. In particular, the first two case studies focus on why the PRC leadership chose to go to war and why they viewed each case as an overall success in spite of tremendous military losses. The Taiwan case study uses the conclusions from the earlier cases to understand and evaluate the possibility of future war with China.

---

[10] Peng Guangqian and Yao Youzhi, eds. *The Science of Military Strategy*, English version (China: Military Science Publishing House, Academy of Military Science of the Chinese People's Liberation Army, 2005) 452. According to the authors this concept is the "quintessence of strategic guidance of China and the Chinese army."

Characteristics of Chinese Thought and Strategic Culture

Does culture matter in the conduct of strategy and warfare? An acultural view would argue that the very nature of war is consistent among all peoples and is best defined by Thucydides' three motivations of "fear, honor, and interest."[11] However, the opposing view would argue culture becomes important in how a people interpret and give meaning or value to those motivations. This section argues in favor of the importance of culture and its associated value system on the strategic culture of China. This section focuses particularly on the differences between Western and Chinese cultural thought and perspectives.

First, one must determine whether there are distinct differences in that way that Westerners and Chinese think and perceive the world. This section draws on psychologist Dr. Richard E. Nisbett's book *Geography of Thought: How Asians and Westerners Think Differently...and Why*, to provide a general overview of the differences between Western and Chinese thought.[12] With his scientific study as a starting point, this study then expands on his research by turning to Dr. D.C. Lau and Dr. Roger Ames's more philosophical study of Chinese thought in their book *Sun Pin: The Art of Warfare*.[13] Lau and Ames's work will segue to the discussion of Chinese strategic culture. In order to describe and define Chinese strategic culture, this section starts with Dr. Alastair Johnston's seminal work, *Cultural Realism: Strategic Culture and Grand Strategy in Chinese History*, and then concludes with Chinese perspectives of their

---

[11] Thucydides, *The Landmark Thucydides: A Comprehensive Guide to The Peloponnesian War*, Robert B. Strassler, ed. (New York: The Free Press, 1976), 43.

[12] Nisbett, Richard E., The Geography of Thought: How Asians and Westerners Think Differently...and Why, (New York, NY: Free Press, 2003).

[13] Lau, D. C. and Ames, Roger T., *Sun Pin: The Art of Warfare*, (New York, NY: Ballantine Books, 1996).

own strategic culture.[14] Finally, this section identifies tensions that are emerging within Chinese culture and briefly discusses how these issues may affect future Chinese strategic culture.

Characteristics of Chinese Thought

What are the characteristics of Chinese thought that distinguish it from Western thought? Due to space constraints, a full discussion of Chinese thought and philosophy is beyond the scope of this monograph. This literature review of Chinese culture focuses on the characteristics of Chinese thought that will help formulate the elements of Chinese Strategic Art. There are two central philosophical concepts which, when combined, interact to form Chinese dialectical thinking.[15] The first is the concept of change, and the second is the concept of the whole.

Nisbett states that there are measureable differences in the way that Westerners and Asians understand and interact with the world around them. The Western approach is reductionist and sees the world as concrete and unchanging. One understands the world by analyzing its many individual parts and categories in search of constant, universal truths or principles. The Chinese approach is holistic and regards the world as a complex, fluid system that one apprehends by examining the relationships between things within the context of the whole system.[16] As a result of this view, the Chinese value experience over logic because from

---

[14] Johnston, Alastair I., *Cultural Realism: Strategic Culture and Grand Strategy in Chinese History* (Princeton, NJ: Princeton University Press, 1995).

[15] Nisbett describes Chinese dialectical thought as focusing on contradictions and "how to resolve them or transcend them or find the truth in both." He adds that the following three principles are essential to understanding the Chinese dialectical approach: the *Principle of Change*, which emphasizes the constantly changing nature of reality; the *Principle of Contradiction*, which states that the constant state of change causes things to have contradictory characteristics such as new and old, or strong and weak; and, the *Principle of Relationship, or Holism*, which states that nothing exists in isolation and that knowing something requires knowing its many relationships. pp 174-175.

[16] Ibid, 141. To illustrate this distinction, Nisbett describes one experiment in which a child must group two objects together from a selection of three illustrations of a cow, a chicken and a patch of grass.

their perspective one cannot know the world solely by observing its parts; one must also actively shape it and interact with it.

Chinese Strategic Culture

Does culture influence strategic preferences? The question of whether culture influences strategic preferences goes back to the early 1950s when academics first investigated the concept of strategic culture. During the Cold War, some Western theorists postulated that there were distinct Soviet cultural assumptions that influenced their strategic preferences. What, then, is a strategic culture? There are many definitions for what constitutes a strategic culture. Johnston defined strategic culture as "an integrated system of symbols (i.e. argumentation structures, languages, analogies, metaphors, etc.) that acts to establish pervasive and long-lasting grand strategic preferences by formulating concepts of the role and efficacy of military force..."[17] Other definitions of strategic culture include concepts such as common narratives, shared beliefs, collective identity, and even the extent to which a country's leaders share a set of beliefs. Johnston, in his book *Cultural Realism*, expanded the concept of strategic culture and applied it to Chinese strategic thought and decision making.

In his study of China's *Seven Military Classics*, Johnston provides evidence of two Chinese strategic cultures: the first was offensive in nature and emphasized the use of violence to resolve security conflicts; and, the second was more diplomatic and emphasized Confucian-Mencian preferences of winning over one's opponent through virtuous actions. Johnston noted

---

American and Western children group the cow and the chicken in a category that represents animals while Chinese children typically group the cow and the grass together because cows eat grass.

[17] Johnston, Alastair I., Cultural Realism: Strategic Culture and Grand Strategy in Chinese History (Princeton, NJ: Princeton University Press, 1995), 36.

that the second approach served either a symbolic means for justifying ancient Chinese strategic behavior or a practical means for deflecting the threat of a more powerful enemy. He then tested his findings by examining strategic decision making during the Ming Dynasty.[18]

Chinese scholars have both challenged Johnston's findings and provided alternative interpretations for explaining Chinese strategic culture. For example, Li Bingyan, a PLA strategist and the former editor of the PLA's *Liberation Army Daily* (*Jiefangjun Bao*) newspaper, offered a Chinese perspective on strategic culture, stating that "Chinese strategic culture defines interest relationships among people, and then turns its field of vision toward expanding various aspects of the relationships among people."[19] Li argues that concepts from the *Book of Changes* heavily influenced early Chinese thought, "It is almost impossible to understand China's cultural system without an understanding of the scheme of *yin* and *yang* and the five elements [water, fire, metal, wood, and earth]."[20] Again, the emphasis in understanding "*yin* and *yang* and the five elements" focuses on interrelationships and not on the thing itself. These concepts placed "greater stress on the mutual inclusion, mutual attraction, and mutual residing of the two sides which are in contradiction."[21] According to the Chinese philosophy of change, nothing is immutable and the weak have an opportunity to become strong just as the strong may become

---

[18] Johnston's selection criteria for a case study were: 1) a period of history where decision makers were self-conscious heirs of the philosophical and textual traditions and experimental legacies out of which the strategic culture emerged; 2) a period where the decision makers are insulated from the effects of foreign or Western strategic cultures; 3) a period where documentation on decision making was relatively rich.

[19] Li Bingyan, "Emphasis on Strategy: Demonstration of Oriental Military Culture," *Beijing Zhongguo Junshi Kexue*, 20 October, 2002, pp 80-85. Open Source Center translation CPP20030109000170, https://www.opensource.gov (accessed 17 March 2010).

[20] Ibid.

[21] Ibid, 80-85.

weak. In this respect, one could argue that ancient Chinese strategists exercised restraint in aggression in order to avoid the inevitable transformation from the aggressor to the victim.

Another scholar, Zhang Tiejun, argues that Johnston deliberately downplayed the influence of Confucian "cultural moralism" on strategic preferences.[22] He states that Ming Dynasty rulers were ethnic Han Chinese who emphasized the Confucian belief of *wang dao* (the way of legitmate kings) in which a ruler gained legitimacy to rule through personal virtue and benevolent conduct. The opposite of *wang dao* was *ba dao* (the way of the illegitimate hegemon), and rulers who abused their power lost their mandate to rule. Zhang adds that this approach applied to both the Ming Dynasty's heartland and the periphery states of the "barbarians." Therefore, according to Zhang, ancient Chinese strategists preferred virtue over violence in order to maintain their legitimacy. However, one must remember that even though Confucianism abhors the use of violence, it permits warfare as a last resort to protect Confucian culture.

It is interesting to juxtapose Western and Chinese descriptions and perspectives of Chinese strategic culture. In the cases above, one sees the cultural predispositions of East and West manifest in the arguments of the different authors. Johnston focuses on an enduring theme which he derives from an analysis of ancient texts and strategic decisions during the Ming Dynasty. Li and Zhang, on the other hand, focus on a more holistic understanding of the relationships between strategic actors.

Culture matters in strategy and the PRC's political and military leadership both appreciate and understand the value of classical Chinese thought. Chinese thought and

---

[22] Zhang, Tiejun, "Chinese Strategic Culture: Traditional and Present Features," *Comparative Strategy*, 21 (London: Taylor & Francis Ltd., 2002), 73-90.

philosophy are integral elements of national identity, which for the CCP is the cornerstone for national unity.[23] In many ways, China's affinity for its own cultural traditions stems from its bad experiences when trying to implement foreign ideas. As Mao cautioned his followers during the Chinese Civil War, one must avoid "cutting one's feet to fit the shoes." This study will use Li and Zhang's more holistic explanations of Chinese strategic culture to later develop the concept of Chinese Strategic Art.

Cognitive Cultural Tensions and Opportunity

The confluence of Western and Asian thought and experience created cognitive tension within Chinese society as early as the Qing dynasty, when China opened up to Western concepts and technology. Peng and Yao describe the late Qing dynasty period as a period of "Chinese and Western Theories Mixing Together."[24] Peng and Yao lament that during this period there was a tendency to blindly copy Western theories and thought while eschewing Chinese traditions and accomplishments. In the other extreme, there was a movement to reject foreign ideas, regardless of their usefulness, in favor of adhering to the traditional way of thinking. Today, globalization exacerbates this tension as technology facilitates greater interaction and information exchange between China and the rest of the world.

---

[23] Peng and Yao, 128. The authors state, "Chinese philosophy values identity and unification" and that the unique Chinese identity influences strategic thinking."

[24] Peng and Yao, 89. The authors highlight the period of the Opium War as a time when foreign invasion "brought about a further fusion of Western strategic theories with strategic theories of ancient China…"

This tension in Chinese identity is not present solely in military circles, but is present throughout Chinese government and academic institutions.[25] For example, the Chinese Academy of Social Sciences (CASS), a research organization in field of philosophy and social science, has fifty research centers that cover 260 disciplines and sub-disciplines, and approximately 4,000 full time researchers.[26] The researchers at CASS and other institutions work "mixing" Western and Chinese ideas to create a new Chinese approach for interacting with the world.[27] Also, the *JOE 2010* document observes that in the last thirty years, the PRC expended great effort to learn from the successes and failures of other nations such as the Soviet Union and Germany.[28]

However, the PRC has not always appreciated its culture and traditions. In the decades following its founding in 1949, the PRC experienced tremendous social turmoil that shook the very foundations of its cultural identity and traditions. Mao's Cultural Revolution and the subsequent mismanagement of the government by the "Gang of Four" following Mao's death ripped apart China's cultural fabric. It was not until 1978, under Deng Xiaoping's leadership, that China gradually regained its pride. With Deng at the helm, the PRC opened its doors to the world and a new flood of foreign ideas such as democracy and capitalism. In 1993, Cui Zhiyuan, a Tsinghua University professor, teaching at MIT, called for a "Liberation of Thought" among Chinese intellectuals, and encouraged them to overcome their fascination and admiration for foreign influences. However, the idea did not take root immediately. It was not until the mid to

---

[25] It is important to note here that unlike the American system that separates the military from the political sphere, in China's current system the PLA is inseparable from the party. In many cases there will be parallel development of organizations and levels in both the political and military structures.

[26] Leonard, Mark, *What Does China think?* (New York, NY: Public Affairs, Perseus Books Group, 2008), 8.

[27] Ibid, 9.

[28] *Joint Operating Environment 2010*, 40.

late 1990s that Chinese intellectuals demonstrated the confidence to create and develop their own ideas. Leonard remarks that intellectuals are now departing from foreign models and seeking new ideas of modernity based on Chinese historical experience and intellectual thought. Gan Yang, a research fellow at the University of Hong Kong's Centre for Asian Studies, described three intellectual periods in China: the Confucian period, the Maoist Era, and the Reformist Period.[29] The challenge that many Chinese scholars and strategists face is how to reconcile these intellectual and theoretical traditions with each other and with the PRC's ever-changing society. An example of the interplay between these traditions is the CCP's use of the Confucian concepts of harmony and virtue to push not only a domestic agenda of political order, but to also to influence the "soft" nature of its foreign policy. An example of this use of Confucian soft power is the worldwide spread of PRC sponsored Confucian Institutes that teach Chinese language and culture to people as far away as West Africa.

There is no doubt that in a country of 1.3 billion people, there are bound to be ideological tensions and contradictions. In some cases, the influx of foreign ideas creates new interpretations of traditional concepts. For example, Yan Xuetong, a Western educated, outspoken and hawkish nationalist stated, "…recently I read all these books by ancient Chinese scholars and discovered that these guys were really smart – their ideas are much more relevant than modern International Relations theory."[30] In particular, Yan was interested in the distinction between two kinds of order mentioned earlier in this paper: *wang dao* and *ba dao*. In his interpretation, the *Wang* system centered on a dominant power and focused inward on maintaining a benign rule over the PRC's provinces and tributary states. The *Ba* system, on the other hand, was a traditional

---

[29] Leonard, 16.

[30] Ibid, 112.

13

hegemonic system imposing its will on the periphery beyond Asia. Yan explained that ancient China used the *Wang* system for relations in Asia and the *Ba* system for barbarians outside Asia. Interestingly, Yan's version of the two systems does not appear to associate the negative connotations with *ba dao* as described by above by Zhang Tiejun. Instead, Yan implies that China should aspire to be a hegemon in order to deal with non-Asian countries such as the US, Europe, and Russia. In any case, Western analysts must bear in mind this dualistic Chinese perspective of foreign relations and understand the emerging changes to its definitions.

Although this paper focuses on the distinctive Chinese cultural approach to strategy, it acknowledges that there are historical and modern currents of foreign influences that inform the evolution of thought in China. These foreign currents, however, do not invalidate the idea of a culturally unique Chinese approach that persisted over time. From a psychological perspective, it is possible for a person to possess both an Asian and a Western identity and to exhibit each under specific circumstances. For example, Nisbett referenced a psychological study of Hong Kong Chinese—who grew up in an environment with strong Western and Chinese traditions—which determined that they could be primed to think either as a Westerner or as an Asian under certain conditions.[31] This idea of cultural priming has interesting strategic implications and may account for some of the ambiguity and contradiction that Western analysts observe in the PRC's strategic outlook. Is it possible to prime a Chinese strategist to think more like a Westerner than as a Chinese? Would there be value in priming him to value Chinese cultural traditions of harmony and relationships? These questions are worthy of further study, but are beyond the limited scope of this monograph.

---

[31] Nisbett, 160.

Chinese Strategic Art

The concept of *Chinese Strategic Art* is a concept derived specially for this monograph to construct a framework with which to understand the Chinese approach to stratagem in war. For the purpose of this study, Chinese Strategic Art is defined as the interaction of Chinese strategic culture with the PLA's *science of strategy*. This section, therefore, will first define the science of strategy as described in the Chinese Academy of Military Science's (AMS) book, *The Science of Military Strategy*. Next, this section will define, in greater detail, the concept of Chinese Strategic Art. Finally, this section will discuss the important relationship between Chinese Strategic art and stratagem.

The science of strategy is "the military science to study the laws of war" which includes the laws which govern the conduct of war and those which govern "strategic evolution."[32] This discipline studies a broad continuum of information that includes historical experience, current circumstances, and predicted future scenarios in order to develop sound strategic decisions and guidance.[33]

The science of strategy is grounded in Marxist strategic theory which emphasizes the development of a scientific strategic theory system to understand the principles of war.[34] The basic approach of Marxist theory is to use dialectical and historical methods to understand the complex systems involved in warfare and politics. According to *The Science of Military Strategy*, the science of strategy "commands operational art and tactics," as it is focused on the larger system as a whole while the operational and tactical levels only address a part of the overall

---

[32] Peng and Yao, 2.

[33] Ibid.

[34] Ibid, 101-102.

system. Although the theoretical system seeks to derive general principles of war and strategy, it is important to note that these principles may change over time as experience and objective conditions change. The theoretical principles of the science of strategy then inform and provide the framework for the development of basic and applied strategic theory. Peng and Yao list the following six characteristics of the science of strategy: practice, politics, comprehensiveness, antagonism, stratagem, and prediction. In short, these principles describe the dynamic, iterative nature of the science of strategy which allows it to change as reality and current circumstances change. They emphasize the importance of combining practice or experience with the Chinese holistic and dialectic approaches to develop stratagems to defeat their adversary. However, the key characteristic of stratagem is buried near the bottom of this list, even though it is the critical component for generating "extraordinary energy from the national strength available and turn the passive to the active."[35] Additionally, Peng and Yao state, "it can be said that science of strategy is a science of wisdom to sum up the laws of using stratagems [sic]."

The Chinese Strategic Art model takes the theoretical system of the science of strategy and combines it with the holistic approach of Chinese strategic culture to derive a qualitative value system to better understand how Chinese strategists generate strategic power through stratagem in order to defeat a superior adversary. This model uses a qualitative value system as opposed to a quantitative system because it is a better fit for the way Chinese strategists evaluate war preparation and performance. In his article "How Beijing Evaluates Military Campaigns: An Initial Assessment," Ron Christman highlights the Chinese preference for qualitative

---

[35] Peng and Yao, 28.

16

assessment by juxtaposing it with the Western preference for quantitative assessment. [36]

Christman states that the Chinese prefer to use "qualitative, subjective assessments when making conclusions about military performance in war," as opposed to the Western approach that makes decisions and evaluations based on "dominant quantitative indicators."[37] He attributes this tendency to a "traditional emphasis in Chinese strategic culture on the battle of 'wits, wisdom, and strategy' being more decisive in determining war outcomes..."[38] Christman's assessment is congruent with the perspectives presented by Peng and Yao in *The Science of Military Strategy*. The PLA authors frequently critique US strategists for their emphasis on military force ratios and technology at the expense of careful appreciation of the overall situation.[39]

When juxtaposed with the Chinese intellectual predispositions identified by Nisbett, one sees how Chinese traditional culture affects Chinese military culture. As mentioned earlier, academics such as Nisbett and Lau highlighted the Chinese predisposition to regard a system in its totality, within the context of the larger environment. Christman supports this philosophical perspective by stating that the CCP leadership emphasizes the importance of "grasping" and "controlling" the "overall strategic situation."[40] In 2002, Qiao Liang and Wang Xiangsui, the two PLA colonels who penned the book *Unrestricted Warfare*, shed light on the Chinese approach to the concepts of "grasping" and "controlling" in an article that they wrote for *Asia Times*

---

[36] Christman, Ron, "How Beijing Evaluates Military Campaigns: An Initial Assessment," *The Lessons of History: The Chinese People's Liberation Army at 75*, eds. Burkitt, Laurie, Scobell, Andrew, Wortzell, Larry M., (Carlisle, PA: Strategic Studies Institute, 2003), 264.

[37] Christman cites Scott Gartner's study of four cases in which Western leaders relied on "dominant quantitative indicators" to evaluate a campaign and determine whether they needed to change their strategy. Scott Garner's study is *Strategic Assessment in War*, (New Haven: Yale University Press, 1997).

[38] Ibid, 265.

[39] Peng and Yao, 135-136.

[40] Christman, 260.

newspaper. [41] They offer two metaphors to explain the Chinese strategic approach: the Chinese Box, and the Buddha's palm. The Chinese box approach, they explain is the practice of attacking "an issue with a framework larger than the issue itself." It is the practice of circumscribing the specific problem into a small mental box, then gradually placing it within boxes of increasing scale and context. In the end, they assert, "you come up with a framework of highest generality to harness the whole situation," and one's potential solutions are sufficiently comprehensive enough to allow the flexibility for maneuver as conditions change in the future. [42]

The second metaphor is that of the Buddha's palm. In the legend of the Monkey King, the Buddha challenged the Monkey King to use his acrobatic skill to escape from the palm of his hand. As the story goes, no matter how hard or far the Monkey King jumped, he could not escape the end of the Buddha's palm. According to Qiao and Wang, this metaphor encapsulates the desire of Chinese strategists to emulate the Buddha's ability to control the superior technological capability of the US military—represented by the masterful and skillful Monkey King. Although at first this metaphor appears very esoteric, Mao Zedong referenced the same analogy in his essay *On Protracted War* to describe a concept of encirclement at the strategic level. [43] According to Mao's interpretation, strategic encirclement of one's enemy is an important condition for victory. Mao wrote:

> Thus there are two forms of encirclement by the enemy forces and two forms of encirclement by our own—rather like a game of *weichi* [italics in the original]…If the game of *weichi* is extended to include the world, there is yet a third form of encirclement as between us and the enemy…The enemy encircles China, the Soviet Union, France and

---

[41] Qiao Liang and Wang Xiangsui, "Chinese-box approach to international conflict," Asia Times, July 31, 2002. http:www.atimes.com/archives/china/dg/31ado1 html (accessed 15 October 2009).

[42] Ibid.

[43] Mao, Zedong, "On Protracted War," *Selected Military Writings of Mao Tse-Tung*, (Peking: Foreign Language Press, 1972), 221.

Czechoslovakia with his front…while we counter-encircle Germany, Japan, and Italy with our front…But our encirclement, like the hand of Buddha, will turn into the Mountain of Five Elements lying athwart the Universe, and the modern Sun Wu-kungs[44]—the fascist aggressors—will finally be buried underneath it…Therefore, if on the international plane we can create an anti-Japanese front in the Pacific region, with China as one strategic unit, with the Soviet Union and other countries which may join it as other strategic units…then that will be our enemy's day of doom.[45]

The example of the weichi game is another example that reiterates the Chinese emphasis on "grasping" and "controlling" the strategic situation as mentioned above. In the opening stages of the game, each player positions his pieces to both set the conditions for his strategic plans while also trying to ascertain his opponent's strategy. The object of a weichi game is to control space on the board by positioning one's forces to encircle the opponent's forces. While a full explanation of weichi is beyond the scope of this monograph, this paper will revisit the analogy later to develop the concept of Chinese Strategic Art.[46]

Chinese Stratagem and *Controlling* the Enemy

Stratagem is the plan or strategy that a Chinese strategist will use to surprise and defeat his adversary. One could argue that the key to stratagem is deception, after all, Sun Tzu did declare at the end of chapter one of *The Art of War* that, "All warfare is based on deception."[47] While this idea has merit, it does not reflect exactly what Sun Tzu meant by deception. From a Western perspective, deception is the act of misleading another person or merely disguising

---

[44] Sun Wu-kung is the Chinese name for the Monkey King.

[45] Mao, 221.

[46] Weichi is also known as "go"—the Japanese name for the same game. For a good introduction to the application of weichi concepts to strategic and operational doctrine, see David Lai's "Learning from the Stones: A Go Approach to Mastering China's Strategic Concept, Shi," (Carlisle, PA: Strategic Studies Institute, 2004).

[47] Griffith, Samuel, B. trans. *Sun Tzu, The Art of War*, (Oxford: Oxford University Press, 1963), 66.

appearances. In US military doctrine, *military deception* describes actions to deliberately mislead the enemy in regards to "friendly military capabilities, intentions and operations."[48] For the Chinese, deception has a more nuanced meaning in regards to controlling one's adversary. In the text that follows Sun Tzu's declaration, he lists various actions that one may take in relation to his opponent and given the existing conditions.[49] The Chinese understanding and execution of stratagem is more fluid and often an emergent response to the constantly changing conditions of the overall strategic situation.

Peng and Yao emphasize the important relationship between stratagem and Chinese strategic thought when they write, "The idea of winning victory by stratagem has always been the main idea of traditional Chinese strategic thinking."[50] In particular, they point out that stratagem emphasizes "use of *limited force* [emphasis added] to achieve victory..."[51] They add that the ideal goals of Chinese strategic thinking are to "subdue the enemy without fighting", to "[win] others over with awesomeness and virtue" and to defeat enemies with "wisdom and stratagem."[52] These ideas are congruent with the PLA's belief that it will be the weaker participant in a conflict and will have to rely on the wisdom[53] and holistic understanding of its leadership to defeat a

---

[48] United Stated Department of Defense, *Joint Publication 3-0, Joint Operations, 17 September 2006 incorporating change 1, 13 February 2008* (Washington, DC: GAO printing, 2008), GL-20.

[49] Griffith, 68-71. Some examples of these actions are: appearing incapable when capable; offering a bait to lure the enemy; feigning inferiority while encouraging the enemy's arrogance; angering the enemy commander if he is prone to anger; and, attacking the enemy where he least expects it.

[50] Peng and Yao, 135.

[51] Ibid.

[52] Ibid, 135.

[53] *Webster's Dictionary* defines wisdom as: 1. the quality or state of being wise; sagacity, discernment, or insight; and, 2. scholarly knowledge or learning. However, this monograph infers that the word wisdom includes a subjective ability to understand the holistic, dialectic nature of a problem. As noted earlier (see footnote 15), the Chinese dialectical approach searches for a middle ground between two contradictions.

stronger opponent. In fact, one may assess that the PLA has no desire to attain the quantitative technological strength or prowess of the US military. The US military, the authors contend, is obsessed with developing military strength and technology that it is unable to incorporate wisdom—Sun Tzu's *The Art of War* in particular—into its doctrine.[54]

No discussion of stratagem is complete without an accompanying discussion of *shashoujian*, commonly translated as the "assassin's mace" or "trump card." Research on the topic of *shashoujian* reveals that it is so broad a term that one could say anything about it and possibly be correct. In 2004, Jason E. Bruzdzinski, then a Senior Professional Staff member of the MITRE Corporation, presented a paper titled "Demystifying *Shashoujian*" before the US-China Commission. He stated that *shashoujian* is a very common idiom in Chinese society and that in general the term refers to "the means or ways by which one overcomes a seemingly insurmountable obstacle."[55] Bruzdzinski adds that *shashoujian* should be considered both as a weapon or weapon system, and as a warfighting concept. This monograph contends that in the context of the arguments presented above, that it is more important to consider *shashoujian* in terms of the larger, holistic context of being a warfighting concept. One should consider whether the Western tendency to focus on military equipment and technology has blinded analysts and academics to the real *shashoujian*: the creative abilities of the PLA strategist. In discussing the development of Chinese military strategy, General Li Jijun, then Vice-President of the AMS, wrote that while technology will influence change in strategy, "[it] will not change the

---

[54] Peng and Yao, 136.

[55] Bruzdzinski, Jason E., as quoted during a testimony before the US-China Commission on 6 February 2004. Downloaded at http://www.uscc.gov/hearings/2004hearings/ written_testimonies/04_02 _06wrts/bruzdzinski html on 27 January, 2010.

fundamental principle that 'people are the decisive factor in the war,' and weapons are but the manifestation of human knowledge."[56]

During a 2008 academic panel on the subject of "The 'People' in the PLA: Recruitment, Training, and Education in China's 80-Year-Old-Military," Roy Kamphausen, of the National Bureau of Asian Research, described a 1999 presentation on America's revolution in military affairs by Dr. Bill Perry, former Secretary of Defense at the PLA's National Defense University. At the end of the presentation PLA General Shali, stood up and stated that all of the military systems and joint capabilities that the US military used during Operation Desert Storm "would have failed without the high-quality, well-trained, and highly motivated soldiers, sailors, airmen and Marines of the United States Military. People are the most important force multiplier."[57]

The Elements of Chinese Strategic Art

This sub-section will describe five elements of Chinese Strategic Art and explain how these elements interact. This sub-section focuses on five elements as opposed to five principles or theories because it is interested in the basic intellectual and cultural building blocks that give rise to the manifestation of Chinese stratagem. To paraphrase Sun Tzu, there may only be five elements of Chinese Strategic Art, but their combinations are limitless.[58] This study will use the

---

[56] Li, Jijun, "Notes on Military Theory and Military Strategy," ed. Michael Pillsbury, *Chinese Views on Future Warfare*, (Washington: National Defense University Press, 1997), 224.

[57] Kamphausen, Roy, as quoted in "The 'People' in the PLA: Recruitment, Training, and Education in China's 80-Year-Old-Military," a panel hosted by the Brookings Institution Center for Northeast Asian Policy Studies and John L. Thorton China Center in cooperation with The National Bureau of Asian Research and the Strategic Studies Institute (SSI) of the U.S. Army War College, (Washington, DC: Brookings Institution, 2008), 8.

[58] In chapter five of *The Art of War*, Sun Tzu discusses the limitless possibilities that arise from combining qi (unconventional) and zheng (conventional forces). To emphasize this point, he says that there are only five musical notes, five colors, and five main flavors, but the combinations of these basic elements or ingredients give rise to innumerable melodies, hues, and flavors.

game of weichi to assist with the description and understanding of these elements of Chinese

Strategic Art. It is important to note, that these elements are not meant to be a reductionist view

of Chinese military theoretical principles—like the US military's joint Principles of War—rather,

they are cognitive tools to better understand the holistic interrelationship between the Chinese

strategist and his adversary or adversaries.

The Five Elements

The primary text that provides the intellectual and philosophical basis for Chinese

Strategic Art is Sun Tzu's *Art of War*. In spite of the many ancient military theorists in China, the

authors of *The Science of Military Strategy* acknowledge Sun Tzu's philosophical and theoretical

legacies to Chinese strategic studies and the science of strategy. In fact, Sun Tzu's principles of

war informed and shaped the development Mao's theory of people's war.[59]

In spite of Sun Tzu's significant contribution to the science and art of Chinese strategy,

there is no formal list or explanation of these basic principles in modern Chinese strategic texts.

One could argue that Chinese strategists internalized these five elements and did not deem it

necessary to enumerate them in a list. However, Sun Tzu does provide a starting point to

discover these five elements. In chapter three of *The Art of War*, Sun Tzu specifies five

conditions that predict victory. These conditions are as follows: he who knows when he can fight

and when he cannot will be victorious; he who recognizes how to use large and small forces will

win; the army whose ranks are united in purpose will be victorious; he who prepares against the

---

[59] Griffith, 45-56.

unprepared will win; and, he whose general receives no interference from the sovereign will win.[60]

The PLA authors of *The Science of Military Strategy* conducted a comprehensive survey of modern and ancient Chinese strategic theories and identified five themes that withstood the test of time. These themes, which reflect Sun Tzu's five conditions, are as follows: stress "Dao (moral influence);" strive for invulnerability by making "the state prosperous and the army strong;" plan deliberately to achieve a complete victory through the "combination of civil and military means;" use stratagem and foreknowledge to attack the enemy where he is weak and catch him by surprise; pay attention to maintaining the army by valuing unity of command, morale and fighting skill.[61]

This study uses Lau and Ames's "philosophical assumptions" of ancient Chinese philosophers to identify and describe the basic elements of Chinese Strategic Art.[62] The end result of this process—which involved combining a couple of Lau and Ames's assumptions such as *strategic advantage* and *weighing with ancient scales*—was the identification of the following five elements: moral virtue (*Dao*), foreknowledge (*Zhi*), dispositions (*Xing*), adaptability (*Bian*), and strategic advantage (*Shi*). Understanding these five elements of Chinese Strategic Art is similar to understanding the five elements mentioned above. While it is important to understand the concept behind each element, it is equally, if not more important to understand the

_____

[60] Griffith, 82-83.

[61] Peng and Yao, 91-92.

[62] The nine philosophical assumptions, according to Lau and Ames are: foreknowledge, the Way, strategic advantage, weighing with the lever scales, battle formation and display, adaptability, yin-yang and a correlative vocabulary, the exemplary commander, and the complete victory, 73-119.

relationships between elements and how they elaborate the relationship between the Chinese strategist and his opponent.

The first element, moral virtue (*Dao*), is the driving force behind Chinese Strategic Art. The Chinese strategist relies on moral virtue to unite the masses and strengthen the unity and resolve of the military toward a common purpose. In Western terms, moral virtue is comparable to developing legitimacy prior to the outbreak of a war. The idea of moral virtue comes from the tradition of "Confucian moralism" where a ruler gains the support of his people through benevolent and virtuous conduct.[63] This concept incorporates the idea of *wang dao* decribed above by Zhang Tiejun. Moral virtue influences not only foreign policy, but internal stability as well. Moral virtue begets military order, discipline, and fighting spirit which then beget initiative and flexibility in maneuvering one's forces to eventually defeat a superior adversary. In the early years of the PLA, the relationship between moral virtue and fighting spirit helped the Communists avoid defeat during the "Long March" and gave them the strength to prevail over the Nationalists in 1949. Fighting spirit continues to be an emphasis in the PLA. In describing the current spirit of the PLA, Wang Xingsheng and Wu Zhizhong write, "The Chinese military's combat spirit can be rated as moving the universe and causing the gods to weep." [64] They elaborate that the PLA developed a "Jingang mountain spirit," a "Long March spirit," a "Shanggan mountain range spirit," an "old Tibet spirit," a "western desert spirit," a "98 flood-fighting spirit," and a "carrying people into space spirit."[65] The authors explain that the fighting

---

[63] Zhang, Tiejun, 76.

[64] Wang Xingsheng and Wu Zhizhong, "PLA Needs to Build Soft Military Power by Strengthening Cohesion, Moral Image," *Zhonguo Junshi Kexue*, 1 January 2007, Open Source Center translation CPP20070621436008. https://opensource.gov (accessed 8 December 2009).

[65] Ibid.

spirit of the PLA is an essential element to the military's hard and soft power—their ability to defeat their enemy with armed force a mere display of power and capability.

The second element, foreknowledge (*Zhi*), emphasizes the importance of knowledge and information in strategic planning and decision making. As mentioned above, the scope of this knowledge is broad and encompasses a holistic appreciation for the larger strategic context of a problem or situation. Foreknowledge includes understanding both subjective and objective conditions and how they interact. Mao called this process of bringing the subjective and objective conditions into "correspondence with each other" the "crux" of being a strategic thinker.[66] However, foreknowledge means more than the collection of facts and data about oneself and one's adversary. Foreknowledge also entails an interaction between two opponents. Lau explains that, "In the Chinese model, 'knowing' is a communal discourse; it is a combination of rhetoric and action, of saying and doing. To 'know' the enemy, then, is to acquire a functional understanding of his particular circumstances while remaining sufficiently indeterminate (wuxing) so that he cannot gain an equal advantage, and then to authenticate this differential in battle."[67]

The third element, disposition or deployment of forces (*Xing*) emphasizes placing one's forces in advantageous positions given the existing conditions: the effects of terrain and weather, and, the location of the enemy. The most critical step in deploying ones forces is to first establish an invulnerable defense before seeking an opportunity to conduct an offensive operation. In chapter four of his *Art of War*, Sun Tzu remarked that "the expert at warfare establishes himself in a position from which he cannot be defeated and does not miss an opportunity to defeat the

---

[66] Mao, 85.

[67] Lau, 74.

enemy."[68] In the modern context of Chinese strategy, this element is the foundation for the PRC's stated strategy of active defense.[69] Two subcomponents to this element are the concepts of emptiness (*wu*) and fullness (*shi*). Successful deployment of one's forces attacks the enemy where he is "empty" or weak, and avoids his strong points.[70] When one has mastered this element of Chinese Strategic Art, the deployment of one's forces will have no discernable form but will be able to concentrate force and energy against the enemy's weakest points. The Chinese strategist will use deployment and disposition of his forces in order to better understand the intent and disposition of his adversary.

The fourth element, adaptability (*Bian*), builds on the other elements described above and involves the transformation from one form or strategy to another in order to adjust to changing conditions. Lau adds, "[*Bian*] is a type of change that is neither rapid nor exhaustive, but gradual, emergent, and characterized by continuity and conservation." The concept is congruent with the changes that occur in the situation or the disposition (*Xing*) of forces in a war. The essence of adaptability is to exploit emerging changes in the overall situation and to seize the initiative against one's enemy. Rather than reacting to an enemy's strategy, the Chinese strategist seeks strategic flexibility in deployment and maneuver in order to *control* his enemy. Through adaptability, the strategist attempts to create the next element, strategic advantage.

---

[68] Griffith, 85.

[69] According to the white paper, *China's National Defense in 2008*, the strategy of active defense adheres to the principle of self-defense and "striking and getting the better of the enemy only after the enemy has started an attack," 10. It combines both offensive and defensive campaigns with the military strategic goal of defending the homeland.

[70] Griffith, 101. Sun Tzu likened this concept to the nature of water which adheres to low ground and has no fixed state or constant form.

The fifth element, strategic advantage (*Shi*) is the ability to transform the subjective and objective conditions of a situation to one's favor. According to Lau and Ames, one cannot study and understand the concept of strategic advantage without also studying and understanding the metaphor of ancient weighing scales (*ch'uan*). Sun Tzu states, "By "strategic advantage" I mean making the most of favorable conditions and tilting the scales in our favor." This image is vitally important to understanding strategic advantage. When one examines the metaphor of the weighing scale, one realizes two meanings: 1) that there is a natural balance of conditions that will favor one side or another; 2) and that one can change the balance in one's favor by adding additional weight or changing the fulcrum of the scale. Lau and Ames state, "Hence, ch'uan means a potential 'opportunity' or 'exigency' that can enable one to upset the balance, alter the status quo, and reconfigure the circumstances."[71]

Shi, in addition to referring to "strategic advantage," may also refer to self cultivation. According to Lau, the etymological root character for *shi* is *yi* which means "to sow, to plant, to cultivate." This secondary meaning for strategic advantage is immensely important as it expresses the important relationship between strategic advantage and the human intellect. Strategic advantage for the Chinese is more than chance and does not necessarily rest with the combatant with the most advanced weapons, or material advantage. In fact, intellectual cultivation becomes the most important element to achieving strategic advantage, especially in a situation of constant change and motion. Sun Pin, reiterating the advice of Sun Tzu, reminds military commanders that, "In the business of war, there is no invariable strategic advantage (*Shi*)

---

[71] Lau and Ames, 93.

that can be relied upon at all times. Every battle and campaign has unique characteristics, qualities and challenges that require new understanding and innovative solutions."[72]

The game of weichi is useful for understanding how a Chinese strategist would apply the five elements of Chinese Strategic Art. In weichi, two players start with an empty board. Unlike chess, there are no predetermined positions for each player's pieces. How one decides to array one's forces is left to the experience, knowledge, imagination and creativity of the individual. As the players interact, campaigns and battle fronts emerge across the board. Unlike in chess, one cannot hope to capture the king nor always plan for swift and decisive victory. Also, whereas in chess different pieces have different values and functions, all the stones in weichi are equal, and gain or lose value by virtue of their disposition. One succeeds by carefully deploying forces and fighting only when necessary. As the players interact and deploy their stones, they attempt to deduce each other's strategy and intent. If the acme of chess is to win in as few moves as possible, then the acme of weichi is to control the board and one's opponent regardless of how little or long it takes.

---

[72] Lau and Ames, 74.

The Application of Chinese Strategic Art

Methodology

This paper uses a qualitative research approach to identify and describe the concept of Chinese Strategic Art and the elements that comprise it. This paper tests the hypothesis that Chinese Strategic Art influences the manifestation of the PRC's strategy in times of conflict with a superior adversary. The author acknowledges the limitations of this heuristic approach; however, he believes that it will be useful in conceptualizing the PLA's approach to future war. This monograph constructs the concept of Chinese Strategic Art by integrating the PLA's science of strategy with the characteristics of Chinese strategic culture. This method provides a framework or lens with which to examine Chinese strategic decisions to enter into a conflict and the decisions during the course of the conflict. The study applies this framework to two historical case studies and one current case study in order to refine the understanding of Chinese Strategic Art.

This paper uses the following selection criteria to identify historical case studies to test the hypothesis:

1. The case study must be a major conflict or war with another nation state.
2. The case study must involve a superpower.
3. Some or all Chinese military campaigns must take place on foreign territory
4. The PRC's leader in each case study must be different.
5. The outcome of the war or conflict was a Chinese victory.

A study of the PLA's military history from 1949 to the present provides only a limited number of case studies with which to apply the concept of Chinese Strategic Art. The major conflicts since the founding of the PRC are as follows: the Korean War, 1950; the Sino-Indian War, 1962; and, the Sino Vietnamese war (also known as the Punitive War by the Chinese), 1979. In addition to these local wars, wars which occurred on China's periphery, there were a number of smaller conflicts involving the islands off of China's coast, to include the showdowns between China and Taiwan in 1958, and 1995 -1996. Of these conflicts, in only two meet the selection criteria listed earlier: the Korean War and the Sino-Vietnamese War. For the contemporary case study, this monograph will use the ongoing Sino-Taiwanese conflict, with particular focus on the period from 2000 to the present.

Each case study will apply the Chinese Strategic Art framework to describe and understand China's strategic approach in each case. The three case studies are: the Korean War, the Sino-Vietnam conflict in 1979, and the Sino-Taiwanese conflict, 2000-present. Applying the Chinese Strategic Art model, one can understand, from a holistic perspective, why Mao decided to enter the war and why the Chinese viewed the end result as a victory for the Communist party. The second case study is the Sino-Vietnam conflict in 1979. Again, the Chinese Strategic Art model helps one understand why Deng Xiaoping decided to go to war and why they viewed it as a success, in spite of the army's poor tactical performance. In the third case study, one sees Jiang Zemin and Hu Jintao's holistic approach to subdue the Taiwanese independence movement without fighting.

The Korean War

The Korean War was the People's Republic of China's first war in the country's modern period. The Korean War is also the case that Chinese strategists use as an example of how an inferior Chinese military can defeat, or at least fight to a draw, a superior, modernized adversary.

The decision to support the Kim Il Sung's North Korean government was a difficult problem for Mao and the rest of the Chinese leadership. Mao's decision to enter into the Korean conflict stemmed from consideration of several conditions. The first condition was the signing of the Sino-Soviet Friendship Treaty on 1 February 1950 in which the Soviets promised to supply China with military advisers and equipment. Not only did the treaty gain the Chinese the promise of modern military equipment, it also bolstered their international position by bringing the US's strategic opponent to their side. The treaty also alleviated Mao's concern with the possibility of being caught between the military forces of the two superpowers, with Soviet troops along the

31

northern border and US troops along the northeastern border with Manchuria. Not only would the possibility of a superpower struggle threaten their sovereignty, but it would also threaten a key industrial area in Manchuria. The CCP determined that they would need approximately three to five years to develop their industry and economic infrastructure and could not afford the possibility of further war within their borders.[73]

Another consideration for Mao was an urgent desire to renegotiate its borders with its neighbors as a step toward establishing China's sovereignty. Also, there was the issue of Taiwan. David Clayton states, "Between 1950 and 1954, the seizure of Taiwan was one of the most important foreign policy objectives for the Chinese People's Government," and there is evidence that the PLA planned to invade Taiwan in early 1950.[74] The US, however, thwarted any PLA invasion plans by moving the 7th Fleet in the Taiwan Straits on 27 June 1950, two days after the North Korean offensive. The US sought to deter the PRC from any military action against Taiwan while the US military was engaged on the Korean peninsula. The PRC immediately denounced the action as an act of aggression against China. Mao perceived the US entrance into the Korean War to be one of many steps to expand US hegemony in the region and achieve strategic encirclement of the PRC. He therefore ordered the massing of additional troops along the border with North Korea and the repositioning of forces to defend a possible attack along the coast adjacent to Taiwan. In fact, the PLA created whole new commands and infantry divisions for the sole purpose of coastal defense.[75] Also at this time, the CCP leadership supported Ho Chi

---

[73] Elleman, Bruce A., *Modern Chinese Warfare, 1795-1989*, (New York, NY: Routledge, 2001), 237.

[74] Ibid, 240.

[75] Zhang, Shugang, Mao's Military Romanticism: China and the Korean War, 1950-1953, (Lawrence, KS: University Press of Kansas, 1995), 48.

Minh's struggle against the French colonialists as a means to create a buffer zone along China's southern border with Vietnam.[76] This deployment of troops at the strategic level was an effort to make China invulnerable to attack, thereby buying time for Mao and the rest of the CCP leadership to deliberate on their next step—which for Mao involved China entering the Korean War.

Between June and October 1950, the military commanders of the 13th Army Corps, deployed along the border, assessed that the American troops feared "being cut off from their communications and retreat lines," and that border forces would train for "close combat battles" and "night operations" to exploit this weakness.[77] Specifically, the 13th Army Corps commanders believe that their forces would be more motivated than US soldiers, and that their combat experience during the 1940s would negate the advantages of the modernized, but less experienced US troops. They also believed that the PLA's flexibility of maneuver and ability to concentrate and disperse forces would defeat their "dull and mechanical" opponent.[78] As the war unfolded and the tide turned against the North Koreans, Mao put his border forces on alert and dispatched a military observation group to North Korea to gather intelligence and develop communications with Kim Il Sung and the North Korean People's Army. On 31 August, 1950, Deng Hua, the commander of the 13th Army Corps positioned along the border, recommended to the Central Military Commission (CMC) that China enter the war only when the US and UN military forces attack north of the 38th parallel. Deng, in keeping with the elements of moral virtue and strategic advantage, considered this to be the best course of action as it would be politically justified and

---

[76] Zhang, Shugang, 69.

[77] Ibid, 62.

[78] Ibid, 76.

attack their adversaries when their forces were stretched out and vulnerable.[79] Based on their

calculations, Deng and his commanders determined that they would adhere to the strategy of

fighting a defensive, protracted war.

On 2 October, 1950, Zhou Enlai sent a warning to Washington via the Indian

Ambassador that China would intervene if US forces crossed the 38th Parallel. The PRC also sent

warnings of possible intervention through London, Moscow, Stockholm, and New Delhi.[80]

However, the US ignored the warning, and on 7 October, UN forces crossed the 38th Parallel, and

by 19 October, occupied Pyongyang. Having failed to deter the UN forces, the PLA infiltrated

forces across the Yalu River between 14 October and 1 November, 1950. After much debate,

Mao convinced the other members of the CCP that it was in China's interest to enter the war and

disrupt US efforts to gain a foot hold in Asia. In his mind it was better to fight the US in 1950

rather than at a later time which would destroy any level of economic development that they will

have achieved.[81]

By the end of 1950, the Chinese People's Volunteers (the nomenclature given to the

Chinese forces in Korea) managed to push US and South Korean forces out of Pyongyang and

south of the 38th Parallel. At the operational level, Peng Dehuai, the overall commander for the

Korean campaign, used stratagem to win initial victories over the quickly advancing US forces.

The PLA had to overcome the initial speed and rapidity with which the US Army operated. Peng

Dehuai decided that instead of racing to engage US forces at the 38th Parallel, a goal no longer

feasible as the US forces attacked early, he would "lure them deep" and force the combat forces

---

[79] Zhang Shugang, 76.

[80] Ibid, 245.

[81] Ibid, 81.

to overextend their logistics capabilities. During combat operations with both US and ROK forces, the PLA commanders applied conventional and asymmetric approaches in an effort to annihilate whole enemy units. By January, 1951, the CPV captured Seoul and pushed the UN troops south of the Han River. However, the CPV, lacking the supplies and equipment of a modern army, surrendered Seoul to the UN forces, now under the command of General Ridgeway, and retreated north of the 38th Parallel.

In January 1951, Peng urged Mao to accept a UN sanctioned ceasefire; Mao refused. Mao believed that China's only option for ensuring its security was to deal the US a decisive defeat. Under Mao's direction, Peng ordered a fourth offensive which culminated by mid-February, 1951. Confronted with a new situation, Mao and Peng decided to adapt their strategy and transition to a protracted defensive strategy characterized by mobile defense. This new approach planned to rotate Chinese combat forces in contact with the enemy in order to preserve their strength while sapping that of the Americans.[82] Mao and Peng also sought to use this strategy to buy time for a political settlement to the conflict. One could argue that had the PLA been mechanized, or at the very least been motorized, they would have been able to deliver a more crushing blow to the coalition. Zhang Shugang states that on several occasions, the ROK mechanized forces were able to avoid encirclement and annihilation because they were able to simply outrun the foot-borne Chinese infantry. In principle, the elements of Chinese Strategic Art enabled a weak military force to fight US and coalition forces to a draw.

---

[82] Zhang, Shugang, 143.

Application of Chinese Strategic Art

From a holistic perspective, the conclusion of the Korean War represented a victory for Mao and the PRC. Mao led the PRC to war against the world's top superpower for two reasons: 1) to establish and strengthen China's relationship with the Soviet Union; and, 2) to disrupt what he perceived to be a US hegemonic strategy for Asia. By improving relations with the Soviets, Mao gained the promise of military and industrial technology. By entering the war against the US, Mao sent a message that China would use military force and accept considerable losses to prevent the threat of strategic encirclement. Not to mention, the CCP leadership used the war to signal the end of what they perceived to be a "century of national humiliation" (1840-1949) in which foreign powers subjugated China.[83] A critical consideration in his decision to go to war was that China had less to lose economically in a war in 1950 to counter US hegemony than later when China's economy would be more developed and the US foothold in the region would be stronger.

In executing their strategy, the Chinese leadership applied an iterative and adaptive approach to neutralize the technological strengths of their opponent throughout out the course of the conflict. Mao and Peng engaged in extensive discourse to examine the nature of the military problem before them. Early on, Mao determined that that PLA would have to rely on what he perceived as their superior fighting to overcome the technological advantage of the US and ROK forces. He and his commanders assessed that the US forces were ideologically weaker and less motivated to fight in the conflict, compared to the PLA. As the PLA was still a peasant army, Mao had to transform the patriotic fighting spirit of the PLA soldier under the conditions of

---

[83] Wortzel, Larry M., "China's Foreign Conflicts since 1949," *A Military History of China*, ed. Graff, David A., and Higham, Robin, (Boulder, CO: Westview Press, 2002), 270

people's war into his *shashoujian*. Interestingly, fifty years later, the idea of people's war as *shashoujian* endures in *The Science of Military Strategy*. In a discussion on the military strategy for the new age, the book refers to people's war as a "magic weapon" which should be studied and applied to modern warfare.[84]

The application of the Chinese Strategic Art framework follows:

Moral Virtue – The PRC justified military intervention in the Korean War as an effort to defend a neighboring state's sovereignty and contest US hegemony in the region. Mao and the rest of the PRC leadership also argued that US naval operation around Taiwan posed a threat to their own sovereignty. Furthermore, the PRC issued warnings through multiple diplomatic channels to inform the US government of the conditions under which the PRC would intervene.

Foreknowledge – As the Korean War unfolded, the PRC sent a military observation group to North Korea to gather information on the situation in Korea. They also developed estimates on US military doctrine which then informed their decision to conduct night operations and close-battles with the enemy. Foreknowledge also applied to understanding their current state development. Mao reasoned that it would be better to fight the US military while the PRC had less to lose economically than in the future when the PRC's focus would be on economic and industrial development.

Dispositions – In preparation for the war, the PRC increased its coastal defenses and built up its forces along the northeastern border. The covert movement of the CPV across the Sino-North Korean border was a masterful execution of this element of Chinese Strategic Art as the CPV positioned itself in a position of advantage to strike an unsuspecting enemy.

---

[84] Peng and Yao, 117.

Adaptability – Mao and Peng demonstrated the ability to adapt throughout the military campaign in order to take advantage of the changing conditions. Early on, the CPV adapted to the faster-than-anticipated movement of the US forces north of the 38th parallel. Later, the PRC leadership changed its focus from a quick, limited war to a protracted campaign in order to position itself for a political settlement.

Strategic Advantage – The PRC leadership created strategic advantage through the buildup of its forces along the northeastern border and their careful, covert infiltration across the border once US and coalition forces crossed the 38th parallel. To use Sun Tzu's metaphor of the crossbow, Mao and Peng created the tension in the bowstring which propelled the arrow into action, catching their adversary by surprise.

The Sino-Vietnamese War, 1979

The Sino-Vietnamese conflict in 1979 is an interesting case because it illuminates the conditions under which it is willing to conduct a local war and how it perceives or measures strategic military success. In the immediate decades following the conflict, many outside observers viewed the conflict as a Chinese failure. The war lasted only three weeks, and, although the PLA captured 6 provincial capitals, they suffered significant losses and left the Vietnamese military largely intact. From a Western perspective, the absence of a decisive victory and failure to demolish the enemy's military equated to military failure. From a Chinese perspective, the war was a strategic success in that it yielded positive results both domestically and internationally.

Domestically, the war helped spur the modernization effort within China, and provided the impetus for military reform and modernization. This military modernization was a necessary step to securing China's long-term security in the region after the Cultural Revolution sapped the spirit of both the PLA and Chinese society as a whole.

Internationally, the war provided China with an opportunity to open up to the West and establish an amenable relationship with the US. The Sino-US relationship was an important condition in preventing what Deng Xiaoping perceived as a Soviet attempt to strategically encircle China. In 1975, PRC aid to Vietnam ceased, and the Soviet Union moved to improve Soviet-Vietnamese relations, resulting in the Soviet-Vietnamese Treaty of Friendship and Cooperation on 2 November1978. This new treaty caused the PRC leadership to fear possible Soviet encirclement, especially since the sixth clause in the treaty stated that the Soviet Union and Vietnam would consult and support each other in the event of an attack, or the threat of an attack.[85] Chinese fears increased in 1978 when Soviet military support and arms shipments to Vietnam increased.

To counter the perceived Soviet threat of encirclement, China's leadership focused on improving its relationships with Japan and the US. The US made an initial overture to Beijing when President Ford visited China in 1975. On 1 January, 1979, the Chinese moved to normalize relations with the US. In response to Chinese overtures to Japan and the US, the Soviets moved to improve their relations with the Southeast Asian countries along China's border.

It is important to elaborate the nuances of the Sino-US-Soviet triumvirate relationship. Michael Marti, a specialist in Chinese national security and foreign policy for the Department of Defense, states that China viewed Soviet support to Vietnam as a threat to his economic plans under the "four modernizations."[86] Deng was concerned that the Soviets would try to derail his

---

[85] Elleman, 288.

[86] Marti, Michael E., China and the Legacy of Deng Xiao Ping, (Washington, DC:Brassey's, Inc., 2002), 11. The four modernizations were, in order of priority: agriculture, industry, science and technology, and national defense.

efforts to modernize China by causing the PRC to worry about defense instead of agricultural and industrial development.

On 17 February, 1979, the PLA began its offensive, crossing the Sino-Vietnamese border at 14 different points. Their commanding officer was Yang Dezhi, a former deputy commander during the Korean War. During the campaign, the PLA performed poorly, due mostly to the overall lack of combat experience of its troops and the lack of logistics and modern equipment. In spite of its shortcomings, the PLA still managed to capture several border cities and provincial capitals, including Lang Son—a critical part of Hanoi's defense. Even though Deng declared early during the fighting that China had no intention of seizing Hanoi, the disposition of PLA forces in Lang Son sent a clear message to the Vietnamese leadership that China could threaten the capital. Almost immediately following the fall of Lang Son on 3 March 1979, the PLA began withdrawal from Vietnam. The PLA completed full withdrawal on 16 March.

The Soviets responded to the Chinese offensive by positioning several naval vessels off the coast of Vietnam. That, however, was the extent of Soviet military participation. The non-existent Soviet military intervention on behalf of the Vietnamese signaled victory to the Chinese leadership.

Application of Chinese Strategic Art

From a holistic perspective, Deng sought to position China between the USSR and the USA in order to provide China the freedom to move toward modernization. On the one hand, he sought to gain access to Western markets and Western technology which, up until then, Washington controlled through the Coordinating Committee on Export Controls.[87] Deng

---

[87] Marti, 10.

believed that he could develop China's relationship with the US by using military force against an enemy the US had fought only a few years earlier: the Vietnamese. On the other hand, Deng sought to normalize relations with the Soviet Union, which had been characterized by antagonism and conflict since the 1960s, thereby eliminating the largest military threat along China's extensive border. By attacking Vietnam, Deng sought to deliver the Soviets a strategic defeat without resorting to a larger scale military conflict with the superpower.

In this case study, one sees Deng's expert combination of the elements of Chinese Strategic Art to attain the overall strategic goal of modernization. His stratagem was to use the punitive war to achieve more advantageous relationships with the two superpowers while assuring China's national security during its period of modernization.

Edward O'Dowd and John Corbett cite a 1997 Academy of Military Science study of the Sino-Vietnamese conflict that assessed the outcome as a resounding success for China[88]. The AMS scholars noted that China's national policy for the war was "strong" and that they achieved all of their campaign objectives (quantified as capturing three provincial capitals, and occupying 21 counties or towns). According to O'Dowd and Corbett, the Chinese academics attributed the difficulties and problems encountered during the campaign to a sundry number of issues to include: lack of combat experience; poor equipment and training; incorrect organization; and the Cultural Revolution. Interestingly, the blame on poor training and equipment mirrored an earlier assessment conducted in 1979. Possibly due to the benefit of time, the new assessment was free to critique the detrimental effects of the Cultural Revolution. However, the authors may have avoided direct critique of Deng's policies as he was still alive.

---

[88] The Military History Section of The Academy of Miltiary Sciences, Zhongguo Renmin Jiefangjunde Qishi Nian, Beijing: Academy of Military Sciences Publishers, 1997) as quoted in O'Dowd Edward C., and Corbett, John F. Jr's essay "The 1979 Chinese Campaign in Vietnam: Lessons Learned.

The application of the Chinese Strategic Art framework follows:

Moral Virtue – The element of moral virtue manifested itself in unique ways during this conflict. On the one hand, Deng secured legitimacy for the war by explaining his logic and intent to punish Vietnam to President Carter. According to various historical sources, President Carter assured Deng of "American 'moral support'" when notified of China's planned punitive war against Vietnam. On 15 February, 1979, Deng declared China's intent to conduct a limited military campaign against Vietnam. On 17 February, 1979, the US Department of State acknowledged the legitimacy of China's invasion of Vietnam, when it stated that the "Chinese invasion of Vietnam was preceded by the Vietnamese invasion of Kampuchea."[89] On the other hand, China displayed its moral virtue in the way that it conducted the war with Vietnam, a historical tributary state with a common Marxist ideology. By limiting their strategic objectives and not capturing Hanoi, Deng Xiaoping sent a message to other periphery states that China did not seek hegemony in the region.

Foreknowledge –Deng and the Chinese leadership employed an iterative approach to carefully examine the nature and relationships of all the strategic conditions that confronted them. In the preliminary stages leading up to the conflict, China faced the possible threat of a war on two fronts—in the north against the Soviets, and in the south against the Vietnamese. Deng moved quickly to normalize relations with the US in order to move the scales in China's favor and counter the possibility of Soviet military intervention. The PRC leadership understood the nature of their Vietnamese adversaries as the PLA provided military advisors to the Vietminh many years earlier during the Indochina war of independence against the French. However, while

---

[89] Chen, King, *China's war with Vietnam, 1979: Issues, Decisions, and Implications*, (Stanford, CA: Hoover Institution Press, 1987), 108.

they may have understood the Vietnamese military, they did not have a good appreciation for the terrain that they fought on. It also appears that the PRC leadership correctly understood the limits of Soviet ability or willingness to use force to support their Vietnamese client state. Unfortunately, PRC intelligence on the Soviets is not currently available to confirm or deny the extent of their knowledge.

Dispositions – Deng warned the Soviets that they would wage a full-scale war in the event the Soviets decided to intervene. To protect its northern border, the China put is forces on emergency alert and established a new command in Xingjiang. It also move over half of its active forces to augment its border defenses. As in the Korean War, the Chinese leadership sought to make China invulnerable to attack prior to launching the offensive in Vietnam. Finally, the PLA demonstrated the essence of this concept by controlling the strategic approach to Hanoi and threatening the capital without actually attacking it.

Adaptability – Deng Xiaoping maintained an adaptive strategy for the Sino-Vietnamese war. By limiting the PRC's strategic goals through official statements, Deng created a window of opportunity for early withdrawal from the conflict. After all, Deng did not want to mire the PRC in a protracted struggle that would drain China's economic resources.

Strategic Advantage – This case study is interesting because the strategic advantage that the PRC gained did not necessarily occur between the PLA and their Vietnamese adversary. Instead, the PRC gained strategic advantage over the Soviet Union, and also gained access to the West through its improved relations with the United States. As mentioned above, Deng sought two objectives: 1) to send the Soviets a firm message that the PRC would use force to prevent strategic encirclement; and, 2) to gain access to Western technology to hasten the PRC's four modernizations.

Chinese Strategic Art and Future War

In 1999, two PLA colonels, Qiao Liang and Wang Xiangsui wrote the book

Unrestricted Warfare, in which they visualized and described future warfare as one which

"transcends all boundaries and limits."[90] Qiao and Wang state that "non-war actions" would

become the new characteristics of future war. In regards to weapons and technology, Qiao and

Wang assert that new concepts for using weapons would be more important than creating

completely new weapons systems. "We believe," the authors state, "The new concept of

weapons will cause ordinary people and military men alike to be greatly astonished at the fact that

commonplace things that are close to them can also become weapons with which to engage in

war."[91] This radical re-conceptualization of warfare was largely the result of the PLA's close

observation and study of the 1991 Gulf War and other US military operations in the 1990s. PLA

officers such as Qiao and Wang realized the unparalleled prowess of the US military in

conventional operations and sought to develop an approach to future warfare, which like the

Buddha's hand would be able to neutralize and defeat a modern, agile adversary. Two years

later, *The Science of Military Strategy* provided ten guiding principles for future high-tech local

war which again emphasized the PRC's intent to fight its own style of warfare with a diverse

combination of military and non-military capabilities.[92]

---

[90] Qiao Liang and Wang Xiangsui, *Unrestricted Warfare*, trans. FBIS (Beijing: PLA Literature and Arts Publishing House, 1999), 8.

[91] Ibid, 17.

[92] Peng and Yao, 452-473. The second principle describes describes five combinations of forces under people's war in modern conditions: 1) regular troops with the masses; 2) regular warfare with guerilla warfare on the sea; 3) "trump card" weapons with flexible strategy and tactics; 4) high-tech weapons with common weapons; and 5) military warfare with political and economic warfare.

The PRC continued to expand on its new concept of warfare during the early 2000s, and drawing on case studies of Japan, Germany, and Soviet Union sought to soften their image in the region and the world as a whole. In 2003, Zheng Bijian, an influential foreign policy thinker, coined the term "Peaceful Rise of China." Other Chinese scholars joined in on this transformation in identity and announced that China would not become another Germany, Japan, or Soviet Union. Instead, China would integrate into the global community and work towards a "win-win" situation for the world. Zheng Bijian later led a research project that studied forty cases in which rising nations failed to achieve their strategic goals when they chose aggressive and expansionist foreign policies. Zheng used this study to provide historical evidence to support China's decision to choose peace over force.[93] According to Leonard, the Chinese recognized that the USSR spent itself into oblivion in trying to match U.S. military power, thus the PRC opted to pursue its asymmetric approach.[94] They are playing a game of weichi versus a game of chess. The softer approach, from the Chinese perspective, is very effective. Shi Yinhong, a liberal internationalist, stated "the U.S. is winning the military game in the Pacific by strengthening its bases…China doesn't like it, but it isn't playing that game. China is playing a different game based on economic investment, trade, immigration, and smile diplomacy. The U.S.A. can't stop this, and it is losing China's game."[95] Part of this effort included creating 100 Confucius Institutes to teach and promote Chinese culture, broadcasting Chinese television in multiple languages, and the opening of its universities to more foreign students than ever before.

---

[93] Leonard, 94.

[94] Ibid, 105.

[95] Ibid.

In the midst of the changing nature of Chinese warfare, the Chinese Strategic Art framework is still relevant to understanding current and future PRC strategy. To illustrate this relationship, this paper will use Taiwan as a case study. In 2001, when Peng and Yao published *The Science of Military Strategy*, the Taiwan issue was the most immediate strategic concern for China. "The Taiwan issue is the largest and last obstacle which we must conquer in Chinese people's path to rejuvenation in 21st century, and it is by all means the most important in our national security strategy in this century."[96] In 2004, the PRC's *China's National Defense* white paper described the Taiwan situation as "grim" and threatened to use armed force to crush any Taiwanese attempts to declare independence.[97] Four years later, however, the PRC's 2008 white paper stated that the Taiwan situation took a "positive turn" for the PRC. Over the course of the last ten years, China successfully applied the five elements of Chinese Strategic Art and waged its new form of warfare in order to control Taiwan's strategic choices and avoid direct military confrontation with the US.

Application of Chinese Strategic Art

From a holistic perspective, the strategies that Jiang Zemin and Hu Jintao have used in regard to Taiwan have been successful. Their continued emphasis on China's modernization and development created a strategic economic advantage that the PRC uses in its relations with the US and Taiwan. Both leaders, especially Hu Jintao, used China's economic influence to strengthen ties with periphery nations and developing nations in South America and Africa in order to counter possible US strategic encirclement. For example, Qiao and Wang, in their *Asia*

---

[96] Peng and Yao, 122.

[97] *China's National Defense* in 2004.

Times article, describe how the Shanghai Cooperation Organization (SCO) provide the PRC with leverage to counter US influence and presence in the Central Asian republics.[98] The PRC leaders also used China's economic influence to diplomatically isolate Taiwan's efforts to gain recognition of its sovereignty.

While the PRC's contemporary strategy is economically focused, the potential still exists that they will again use military force to affirm its growing power and influence in the region. Although the CCP leadership states that the PRC only uses military force for self-defense,[99] the case studies presented above indicate otherwise. In both the Korean and Vietnamese cases, the PRC used military force to influence its strategic relationship with a "barbarian" power. Therefore, it is likely that the PRC will use military force in the future to affirm a new relationship of authority and strength between it and the rest of world. Why has China not flexed its military muscle at a time when the US is relatively weak? It is possible that Hu Jintao and the CCP leadership do not believe they have achieved the invulnerability that Sun Tzu insisted upon. For example, China's economy is still closely tied to the US economy, and the CCP continues to battle internally divisive forces of separatism, extremism, and terrorism.[100] Any attempt to unseat the US from its hegemonic position would likely have negative consequences on China's economy and would embolden the divisive internal forces to challenge the legitimacy of the CCP. Not to mention, the CCP still considers the PRC to be in "a stage of economic and social

---

[98] Qiao and Wang, "Chinese-box Approach to International Conflict."

[99] Wortzel, 268.

[100] *China's National Defense in 2008*, 5.

transition."[101] The CCP's first concern is social stability and it considers *wang dao* as the appropriate approach to achieve that goal.

The application of the Chinese Strategic Art framework for the Sino-Taiwanese conflict follows:

Moral Virtue – Chinese thinkers and policy makers made efforts to soften the image of China's rise to the outside world. In November 2009, Hu Jintao officially adopted the foreign policy platform of "constructing a harmonious world" and working toward "joint development" and "shared responsibilities."[102] This marked the first time a Chinese leader presented a "comprehensive set of theories with an international perspective."[103] Earlier in 2006, the Chinese developed a "win-win" strategic approach, which they formally adopted in the 2006 *China's National Defense* white paper. On might infer from these official policies that the PRC's current leadership is invested in pursuing a *wang dao* approach to the world—or at least the developing world and China's periphery[104]—and setting the stage to legitimate China's leadership in world affairs. Also during this time, the PRC increased its involvement in United Nations (UN) Peacekeeping operations and even set up a civilian police peacekeeping center called the China Peacekeeping CIVPOL Training Center in 2003.[105] All these efforts are focused on developing

---

[101] China's National Defense in 2008, 6.

[102] Lam, Willy, "Hu Jintao Unveils Major Foreign-Policy Initiative," China Brief, vol IX, issue 24, December 3, 2009,
http://jamestown.org/programs/chinabrief/archivescb/cb20090/?tx_publicationsttnews_pi2%5Bissue%5D=24 (accessed 10 December, 2009), 2.

[103] Ibid.

[104] Ibid. Citing a *Wall Street Journal* article on 28 November, 2009, Lam writes that China "led developing nations including India and Brazil in pressing the industrialized world to devote at least 0.5 percent of GDP to helping poor nations in areas including fostering green technology," 3.

[105] He, Yin, "China's Changing Policy on UN peacekeeping Operations," *Asia Paper*, July 2007 (Stockholm: Institute for Security and Development Policy, 2007), 43

the CCP's legitimacy to rule over all its territory, including Taiwan. According to Murray Scott Tanner, an analyst for RAND Corporation, the PRC's efforts are aimed at changing Taiwanese attitudes to one comprised of anti-independence and political acceptance of the PRC.[106]

Foreknowledge – As mentioned above in the introduction, in 2000 the PLA had more senior level officers studying at American graduate programs than the US military. The purpose of this emphasis on Western graduate education may be two-fold: first, to better understand the strategic thinking of the US; and, second, to develop senior leaders who can lead forces in modern, informationalized conditions. On the clandestine side of foreknowledge, the PLA intelligence services and other PRC government agencies have extensive spy networks in foreign countries to collect strategic information, technology information, and information on groups that pose threats to the PRC's internal stability.[107]

Dispositions – It is not sufficient to solely examine the dispositions and deployment of PLA units and equipment. One must expand the focus to include the worldwide disposition of Chinese businesses and economic infrastructure as well. The *Science of Military Strategy* discusses the evaluation of "war potential" in non-military capabilities and resources. The term "war potential" describes the inherent potential of an economic, civil, or political resource in supporting the military in times of war. Given China's extensive integration into the world economy, and the plethora of Chinese communities worldwide, China does not need to establish military bases or forces overseas the way that they US does because the other Chinese instruments of national power are able to transform into war potential to support the future vision

---

[106] Tanner, Murray S., *Chinese Economic Coercion Against Taiwan: A Tricky Weapon to Use,* (Santa Monica, CA: RAND Corporation, 2007), 105-106.

[107] *China's National Defense 2008*, identifies these groups as separatist forces working for "Taiwan independence," "East Turkestan independence," and "Tibet independence," 6.

of people's war. In fact, PLA plans in the late 1990 for invading Taiwan included the mobilization of large numbers of civilian cargo ships to transport the large force required to seize the island.[108] The PRC also used its participation in UN peacekeeping operations to influence "pro-Taiwan" governments to abandon recognition of the Republic of China.[109] In addition to these approaches, the PLA built up its asymmetric strength with military cyber capabilities, and modernized coastal defenses and missile capabilities along the Taiwan Strait. The strategic aim of these asymmetric capabilities is to neutralize the conventional US military forces that would come to Taiwan's aid in the event of a war with the PRC.

Adaptability – The concept of "war potential" described above also applies in this category. The PLA focuses on developing capabilities and resources that have both military and non-military uses and characteristics. The PRC's approach to pro-independence efforts in Taiwan included a flexible use of economic incentives and threat of armed force to influence Taiwan's influential business community. Over the last decade, for example, the PRC gradually integrated Taiwan's economy to the point where Taiwan's economy is dependent on the Chinese market.[110]

Strategic Advantage – The PRC generated cumulative national power to include economic, political, military, and cultural power to give them a strategic advantage over Taiwan and the US. In terms of military capabilities, the PRC developed strategic missile and cyber capabilities as a possible means to neutralize US military intervention in the event of a Sino-

---

[108] Yuan Lin, "PLA Capabilites in Dealing with Taiwan," Hong Kong *Kuang Chiao Ching* No.299 in Chinese, 25 September 1997, Open Source Center translation FTS19970925000679. https://opensource.gov (accessed 31 March 2010).

[109] *China's National Defense in 2008*, 6.

[110]Tanner, 135.

Taiwanese crisis. At the diplomatic level, the PRC is trying to achieve a strategic encirclement of the government of Taiwan by attacking its diplomatic relationships.

Conclusion

The goal of this monograph was to contribute to the subjective understanding of Chinese strategic thought and decision making by constructing a conceptual framework to apply to Chinese strategic thought and action. The impetus for this qualitative study was the ambiguity that surrounds American understanding of the PRC's strategic intentions. The end result of this study was the creation of the Chinese Strategic Art framework which included five key elements of Chinese strategy that persisted over time. The Chinese Strategic Art concept involved developing a holistic understanding of the overall strategic situation and then using that knowledge to control one's adversary.

The paper presents the following conclusions in regards to modern Chinese strategy. While the PLA pursues Western-style modernization of its organization, equipment, and doctrine it will retain distinctive Chinese approach to strategy that draws from China's rich intellectual traditions and experiences from the dynastic periods to the modern era. Over the last 60 years, China contended with various external and internal threats and their strategic approach adapted accordingly. The last major conflict that involved PLA ground forces occurred in the 1979 Sino-Vietnamese War and ended after only three weeks of combat. Since then, China made concerted efforts to transform its image from a monolithic socialist machine to a Chinese system with a mix of socialist and traditional (Confucian, Taoist, Legalist) characteristics. However, one must not be distracted by assertions that the PRC's strategy focuses on self-defense and seeks harmonious peaceful relations with all its neighbors. In reality, the PRC's leaders have used force to build and affirm new relationships between China and "barbarian" superpower. The PRC participated in the Korean War in order to enhance its relationship with the Soviet Union and gain access to important technology. Later, in 1979, the PRC used military force against Vietnam in order to change its relationship with the Soviets and build a new relationship with the US. In the future, the PRC will likely use military force in a limited conflict to establish itself a world leader with global interests and capabilities. For the time being, however, the CCP's leadership is most concerned with internal social stability and will continue to the *wang dao* approach to guide its relations with the rest of the world.

The Chinese leadership is aware of how times and conditions have changed since birth of the CCP and its revolutionary spirit. The past eighty-two years tempered the revolutionary fervor and forced Chinese scholars and leaders to research new means for maintaining social order and the rule of the party. Understanding China's intense concern for internal stability and the characteristics of Chinese Strategic Art, as defined in this monograph, reveals new insight into the primary focus of China's military modernization efforts. The true measure of the PLA's strength and capability does not emerge from counting the number of Type-99 tanks or operational level missile systems. The real measure of capability lies in understanding the system of education and intellectual cultivation of its soldiers and officers. If the Chinese learned nothing else over the last 5,000 years, they understand the true value of the human element in the creative expression of stratagem and warfare.

Clausewitz once described warfare during the Napoleonic era as a contest between two wrestlers, each trying to use physical force to "compel the other to do his will..." While that was a fit description of warfare in his era, it does not adequately describe warfare in regards to the PRC. A better metaphor for China would be a contest between a Chinese Taijiquan master and a Western mixed-martial arts opponent.[111] Although the Western opponent may have some skills derived from Asian fighting styles, he seeks victory by applying size, strength, and speed to pummel his opponent or force him into submission. The Taijiquan master, on the other hand,

---

[111] Taijiquan—which translates as supreme ultimate fist—is a style of martial arts that emphasizes softness to overcome hardness, and focuses on internal energy instead of external, physical force. There is no equivalent to Taiji in Western pugilistic systems. Mixed-martial arts, is a pugilistic sport much like boxing, however the combatants are allowed to use a greater repertoire of skills such as kicks and ground fighting.

being older and inferior in physical strength relies on wit, wisdom, and stratagem to use his opponent's strength against him.

Finally, the study of Chinese Strategic Art is beneficial to US military officers and strategists as it not only expands understanding of the PRC's strategic decision making, but may also complement US strategic thinking. As mentioned in the introduction, there is a pronounced gap between the level of US understanding of Chinese strategy and the level of Chinese understanding of US strategy. The Chinese are learning about US strategy faster than Americans are learning about the Chinese approach to strategy. They are carefully studying modern strategic approaches and selectively combining them with the wisdom of traditional Chinese thought on strategy. As a result, Chinese strategists may be developing new strategic ideas and concepts that will provide them with a strategic asymmetric advantage over a technologically superior US adversary in the future. It is imperative that US military officers and strategists understand the culturally distinctive Chinese strategic approach beyond rudimentary quotations from Sun Tzu and Mao Zedong. Otherwise, US military officers and strategists will run the risk of misunderstanding and miscalculating Chinese strategy by "mirror imaging" Chinese strategic preferences and calculations with Western norms and values. Only a strong understanding of Chinese Strategic Art will help the US military leap beyond the reach of the Buddha's palm.

In the introduction, this monograph invoked a Chinese proverb that states "stones of other hills may serve to polish the jade of this one." The author hopes that this monograph serves as a starting point for further study of not only Chinese strategic theory and thinking, but US military strategy in general.

BIBLIOGRAPHY

Bjorge, Gary J. *Moving the Enemy: Operational Art in the Chinese PLA's Huai Hai Campaign*, Ft. Leavenworth, KS: Combat Studies Institute, 2004.

Boorman, Scott A., *The Protracted Game: A Wei Chi Interpretation of Maoist Revolutionary Strategy*, New York, NY: Oxford University Press, 1969.

Chen, King, *China's war with Vietnam, 1979: Issues, Decisions, and Implications*, Stanford, CA: Hoover Institution Press, 1987.

Christensen, Thomas J., *Useful Adversaries: Grand Strategy, Domestic Mobilization, and Sino-American Conflict, 1947-1958*, Princeton, NJ: Princeton University Press, 1996.

Christman, Ron, "How Beijing Evaluates Military Campaigns: An Initial Assessment," *The Lessons of History: The Chinese People's Liberation Army at 75*. Edited by Laurie Burkitt, Andrew Scobell, and Larry M. Wortzell, Carlisle, PA: Strategic Studies Institute, 2003.

Elleman, Bruce A., *Modern Chinese Warfare, 1795-1989*, New York, NY: Routledge, 2001. *A Military History of China*. Edited by David A. Graff and Robin Higham. Boulder: Westview Press, 2002.

He, Yin, "China's Changing Policy on UN peacekeeping Operations," *Asia Paper*, July 2007, Stockholm: Institute for Security and Development Policy, 2007.

Hood, Steven J., *Dragons Entangled: Indochina and the China-Vietnam War*, Armonk, NY: M.E. Sharpe, 1992.

Information Office of the State Council of the People's Republic of China. *China's National Defense in 2000.* http://www.china.org.cn/e-white/2000/index.htm (accessed 10 January 2010).

--------. *China's National Defense in 2002.* http://www.china.org.cn/e-white/20021209/index.htm (accessed 10 January 2010).

--------. *China's National Defense in 2004.* http://www.china.org.cn/e-white/20041227/index.htm (accessed 10 January 2010).

--------. *China's National Defense in 2006.* http://china.org.cn/english/features/book/194421.htm (accessed 10 January 2010).
.
--------. *China's National Defense in 2008.* http://merln.ndu.edu/whitepapers/China_English2008.pdf (accessed 18 October 2009)

Johnston, Alastair I., *Cultural Realism: Strategic Culture and Grand Strategy in Chinese History*, Princeton, NJ: Princeton University Press, 1995.

Lai, David, "Learning from the Stones: a Go Approach to Mastering China's Strategic Concept, Shi," Carlisle Barracks, PA: Strategic Studies Institute, U.S. Army War College, 2004.

Lam, Willy, "Hu Jintao Unveils Major Foreign-Policy Initiative," China Brief, vol IX, issue 24, December 3, 2009, http://jamestown.org/programs/chinabrief/archivescb/cb20090/?tx_publicationsttnews_pi2%5Bissue%5D=24 (accessed 10 December, 2009)

Lau, D. C. and Ames, Roger T., *Sun Pin: The Art of Warfare*, New York, NY: Ballantine Books, 1996.

Li Bingyan, "Emphasis on Strategy: Demonstration of Oriental Military Culture," *Beijing Zhongguo Junshi Kexue*, 20 October, 2002.   Open Source Center translation CPP20030109000170, https://www.opensource.gov (accessed 17 March 2010).

Li, Jijun, "Notes on Military Theory and Military Strategy," ed. Michael Pillsbury, *Chinese Views on Future Warfare*, Washington, DC: National Defense University Press, 1997.

Marti, Michael E., *China and the Legacy of Deng Xiao Ping*, Washington, DC: Brassey's, Inc., 2002.

Nisbett, Richard E., *The Geography of Thought: How Asians and Westerners Think Differently...and Why*, New York, NY: Free Press, 2003.

Peng Guangqian and Yao Youzhi, eds. *The Science of Military Strategy*, English version, China: Military Science Publishing House, Academy of Military Science of the Chinese People's Liberation Army, 2005.

Qiao, Liang and Wang Xiangsui, *Unrestricted Warfare*, Washington, DC: Foreign Broadcast Information Service, 2000.

Qiao Liang and Wang Xiangsui, "Chinese-box approach to international conflict," Asia Times, July 31, 2002. http://www.atimes.com/archives/china/dg/31ado1.html (accessed 15 October 2009).

Ryan, Mark A., *Chinese Warfighting: the PLA experience since 1949*, Armonk, NY: M.E. Sharpe, c2003.

Scobell, Andrew, *Civil-Military Change in China: Elites, Institutes, and Ideas after the 16th Party Congress*, Carlisle Barracks, PA: Strategic Studies Insititute, U.S. Army War College, 2004.

Sun Tzu. *The Art of War*. Translated by Samuel B. Griffith. Oxford: Oxford University Press, 1963.

Tanner, Murray S., *Chinese Economic Coercion Against Taiwan: A Tricky Weapon to Use*, Santa Monica, CA: RAND Corporation, 2007.

United States Department of Defense, *Annual Report to Congress: Military Power of the People's Republic of China 2008*, Washington, D.C.: Office of the Secretary of Defense, 2008.

United Stated Department of Defense, Joint Publication 3-0, Joint Operations, 17 September 2006 incorporating change 1, 13 February 2008, Washington, DC: GAO printing, 2008.

United States Joint Forces Command (JFCOM), *The Joint Operating Environment 2010: Challenges and Implications for the Future Joint Force*, Suffolk, VA: JFCOM, Center for Joint Futures, 2010.

Wang Xingsheng and Wu Zhizhong, "PLA Needs to Build Soft Military Power by Strengthening Cohesion, Moral Image," *Zhonguo Junshi Kexue*, 1 January 2007. Open Source Center translation CPP20070621436008. https://opensource.gov (accessed 8 December 2009).

Whiting, Allen S., *The Chinese Calculus of Deterrence: India and Indochina*, Ann Arbor, MI: University of Michigan Press, 1975.

Wortzel, Larry M., "China's Foreign Conflicts since 1949," *A Military History of China*, Edited by Graff, David A., and Higham, Robin, Boulder, CO: Westview Press, 2002.

Yuan Lin, "PLA Capabilites in Dealing with Taiwan," Hong Kong *Kuang Chiao Ching* No.299 in Chinese, 25 September 1997, Open Source Center translation FTS19970925000679. https://opensource.gov (accessed 31 March 2010).

Zhang, Shugang, *Mao's Military Romanticism: China and the Korean War, 1950-1953*, Lawrence, KS: University Press of Kansas, 1995.

Zhang, Tiejun, "Chinese Strategic Culture: Traditional and Present Features," *Comparative Strategy*, 21, London: Taylor & Francis Ltd., 2002.

www.ingramcontent.com/pod-product-compliance
Lightning Source LLC
Chambersburg PA
CBHW081748280526
45789CB00008B/2780